Original title:
When We Fell Apart

Copyright © 2024 Swan Charm
All rights reserved.

Author: Liisi Lendorav
ISBN HARDBACK: 978-9916-89-985-4
ISBN PAPERBACK: 978-9916-89-986-1
ISBN EBOOK: 978-9916-89-987-8

The Shadow of Togetherness

In the quiet night we stand,
Hands entwined, a soft command.
Whispers floating on the breeze,
Hearts as one, a gentle tease.

Stars above twinkle in sight,
Guiding dreams, our shared delight.
Moonlit paths where we do roam,
In each other's arms, our home.

Through the storms, we face the dance,
Every struggle, a second chance.
Laughter brightens the darkest hour,
Together we bloom, purest flower.

Yet shadows linger, fears may creep,
In every promise, secrets we keep.
But trust withstands the weight of night,
In the dark, your love's my light.

So hand in hand, let's forge ahead,
With every step, our spirits fed.
In every heartbeats' soft caress,
We find strength in togetherness.

The Language of Empty Rooms

Silence whispers in corners,
Echoes of laughter now gone,
Dust settles on old memories,
Time lingers, a forgotten song.

Shadows dance on the wall,
Flickering, fleeting, then still,
The heart beats in solitude,
Wishing for warmth, longing for thrill.

Windows gaze at the street,
Unseen stories drift by,
Curtains drawn tight in repose,
Underneath a clear, blue sky.

Footsteps fade into night,
A soft sigh breaks the calm,
Each room holds its own tales,
Wrapped in the air, like balm.

Hope flickers like a candle,
In a space both vast and small,
Rooms may be empty today,
But the memories still call.

Colder than Yesterday

Morning frost bites gently,
Chill wraps the earth anew,
Whispers of autumn linger,
As shadows stretch and skew.

Bare branches softly tremble,
Underneath the muted sky,
Breath hangs in frozen moments,
As time slips quietly by.

Nights grow long and restless,
Stars flicker, dim, and fade,
Each second feels eternal,
In the silence, memories wade.

The warmth of laughter fades,
In echoes of yesteryear,
Promises once gently spoken,
Now lost in winter's sphere.

Hope shivers in the stillness,
Yet embers can still glow bright,
For every night that's colder,
Leads to dawn's soft, warming light.

Shattered Reflections

Fragments of a broken dream,
Scattered on the cold, hard floor,
Each piece tells a story,
Of what there was before.

Mirrors no longer hold truth,
Only ghostly silhouettes,
Fleeting moments of laughter,
Now shrouded in regrets.

Time's cruel hand has broken,
What once felt whole and right,
Shadows stretch and linger,
In the depths of the night.

Eyes search for the pieces,
Hoping to find the way,
But the shards remain scattered,
In a cold, distant sway.

Yet through the cracks, a glimmer,
A spark of light shines through,
In shattered reflections lie,
Hidden paths to renew.

Collapsing Canvases

Colors bleed into darkness,
As brushes fall to the floor,
Art once vibrant and lively,
Now whispers tales of yore.

Each canvas holds a story,
Of visions boldly cast,
Yet time erodes the edges,
As dreams become the past.

Strokes that once danced with fervor,
Now dripped in uncertainty,
Emotions scream from the fibers,
Yearning to break free.

In the chaos of color,
Beauty fights to remain,
Even as the frame falters,
Amidst the falling rain.

But in the depths of discord,
New patterns may arise,
From the collapsing canvases,
A phoenix in disguise.

Unraveled Dreams

In twilight's hush, the shadows creep,
Whispered wishes, secrets deep.
Threads of hope begin to fray,
Unraveled dreams, they slip away.

Stars above, a distant guide,
Each ambition, love, and pride.
Yet in silence, fears reside,
Unraveled dreams, we cannot hide.

Once bright visions fade to gray,
Slipping slowly, day by day.
Yet in the quiet, hearts will sway,
Unraveled dreams must find their way.

Through the night, we seek the dawn,
With every loss, new paths are drawn.
In every tear, a chance to play,
Unraveled dreams will lead the way.

In fractured hopes, we find our strength,
In every setback, a new breadth and length.
Though fragile threads may lead astray,
Unraveled dreams still hold their sway.

Lost in Translation

Words fall softly, like autumn leaves,
A tender touch, but nothing cleaves.
Between the lines, the meaning hides,
Lost in translation, where love divides.

Silent echoes of things unsaid,
Bridges built, but slowly shred.
In tender glances, worlds collide,
Lost in translation, hearts reside.

The laughter fades, the tears arise,
A gentle truth beneath the lies.
In every sigh, a whispered guide,
Lost in translation, where dreams abide.

Fingers trace the path once found,
With each heartbeat, a longing sound.
In the distance, a yearning stride,
Lost in translation, love's wild ride.

Yet in the chaos, hope persists,
A flash of light through morning mist.
Though languages may try to hide,
Lost in translation, souls collide.

Bitter Sweetness

In every joy, a hint of pain,
A bittersweet embrace remains.
Laughter dances, sorrow weaves,
Bitter sweetness, the heart deceives.

Memories linger, soft and bright,
Yet shadows dance in fading light.
With every smile, a tear departs,
Bitter sweetness, the art of hearts.

Through every sunset's vibrant hue,
A tinge of gray, the twilight blue.
In every love, a chance to mourn,
Bitter sweetness, forever born.

Time moves on, yet treasures stay,
In quiet moments, we find our way.
Through every choice, an ache resides,
Bitter sweetness, where life confides.

But still we chase the fleeting bliss,
In tender moments, a stolen kiss.
Though life may teach, we will abide,
Bitter sweetness, our hearts' true guide.

Echoes of Yesterday

In quiet rooms, the past remains,
Whispered secrets, silent chains.
Memories echo through the halls,
Echoes of yesterday, haunting calls.

Footsteps linger, shadows play,
In faded dreams, we drift away.
Through time's embrace, history sprawls,
Echoes of yesterday, timeless thralls.

Yet in the stillness, light will break,
A dawn arising, fresh paths to take.
In every heartache, a lesson sprawls,
Echoes of yesterday, life enthralls.

Turning pages of lives once lived,
Stories woven, and love that gives.
In every heartbeat, nothing stalls,
Echoes of yesterday, life's sweet brawls.

So let the past be not a ghost,
But a guiding light, our hearts can boast.
For in each echo, wisdom calls,
Echoes of yesterday, love enthralls.

Whispers of Distance

In the quiet night, shadows play,
Stars above seem far away.
Hearts once close, now out of reach,
Words like wind, they're hard to teach.

Echoes linger in the dark,
Memories glow like a fleeting spark.
Time drifts slowly, like the tide,
A gentle pull we cannot hide.

Familiar faces fade from view,
Yet whispers linger, soft and true.
When silence speaks, we understand,
Distance grows, yet still we stand.

A love once strong, now wears thin,
Through every loss, we learn to win.
Not all journeys end in despair,
Some survive on whispered air.

Ghosted Promises

In the light of day, they fade away,
Promises made seem far astray.
Whispers linger, yet remain unheard,
Ghostly echoes of a broken word.

Under twilight's veil, dreams take flight,
But shadows creep in the long night.
A single touch, now a distant thought,
In the silence, we find what we sought.

Hope like a candle flickers bright,
Yet doubt floods in, stealing its light.
Every vow feels like a sigh,
In the absence, we learn to fly.

Promises ghosted, left in the past,
The heart holds on, but breaks so fast.
What once was gold, now turns to dust,
In haunted halls, we place our trust.

Fraying Ties

Threads of connection, worn and thin,
Each argument feels like a sin.
Words once woven into a song,
Now unravel where we don't belong.

Through laughter shared and tears that fell,
We built a bond, a sacred shell.
But storms arose, and tempests blew,
Fraying ties now bid adieu.

Once hand in hand, now drifting apart,
Time's cruel toll weighs heavy on the heart.
What was vibrant is now too tight,
Held together by sheer will and fight.

Yet hope remains in the tangled thread,
With gentle pulls, some words unsaid.
In the quiet, we find our way,
To mend the ties that fray each day.

The Last Embrace

In the fading light, we draw near,
The last embrace is filled with fear.
Memories flash, bright yet brief,
A bittersweet touch, mingled grief.

Skin against skin, a final hold,
Stories whispered, soft and old.
Promises linger in the air,
In this moment, do we dare?

The world blurs, as we let go,
Hearts intertwine in ebb and flow.
A sigh escapes, like a tender breeze,
The last embrace, a quiet tease.

As shadows stretch, we'll drift apart,
Yet carry echoes in our heart.
In every ending, love finds its grace,
Memories held in the last embrace.

Fragments of Us

In whispers soft, we shared our dreams,
Caught in time's fleeting, fragile seams.
Echoes linger in silent air,
Moments woven with tender care.

Scattered pieces, a puzzle unsolved,
In each heartbeat, our love evolved.
Through distant lands, our paths entwined,
In every fragment, the heart defined.

A sunset glow paints memories bright,
Reflections blend in fading light.
Soft murmurs wrap around the night,
In the stillness, we take flight.

The laughter shared, the tears that flow,
A tapestry of joy and woe.
While time may shift and worlds may part,
In these fragments, you hold my heart.

Remnants of Laughter

In jovial halls, laughter rang clear,
Moments cherished, dance with cheer.
Echoes of joy in the evening glow,
Where fond memories continue to grow.

Tickled fancies and playful sighs,
Under the starlit, endless skies.
A gentle whisper, a playful tease,
In every chuckle, sweet memories freeze.

Fragments of joy, scattered like sand,
Golden sands slipping through hand.
Remnants of laughter, soft and bright,
Can make the darkest moments ignite.

With every giggle, a story unfolds,
In laughter's warmth, the heart beholds.
Oh, to hold each whisper dear,
For in laughter, we find our cheer.

Worn Pages

Tattered edges, stories unfold,
In every crease, secrets bold.
Worn pages whisper tales of the past,
Moments cherished, shadows cast.

Ink stains linger, memories seep,
In quiet nights, they softly creep.
Turn the leaves, see time's embrace,
In every word, a forgotten place.

Faded thoughts in margins lie,
Dreams suspended, each sigh a sigh.
Worn pages hold the lives we've led,
In ink and paper, the heart is fed.

In fragile light, we relive our tales,
Through winds of change and gentle gales.
History etched in silent screams,
On worn pages, we chase our dreams.

Shadows of What Was

In twilight hues, shadows arise,
Fading whispers, soft goodbyes.
Memories linger, a distant call,
In echoes of laughter, we rise and fall.

The silence stretches, a haunting tune,
Remnants lingering beneath the moon.
In shadows, stories weave and sway,
Of love once bright, now worn away.

Ghostly figures dance on the wall,
Flickers of joy then rise and fall.
In shadows cast, we find our fear,
Yet in their depth, truth draws near.

What was once vibrant now holds a sigh,
Fleeting moments that softly fly.
In the embrace of twilight's grace,
Shadows remind us of time's embrace.

The Art of Letting Go

In gentle whispers of the night,
I learn to fade, to lose the fight.
Each memory, a fragile thread,
I weave in silence, let them tread.

With open hands, I free my soul,
Releasing all that took its toll.
A step away from shadows cast,
I find the light where pain was vast.

The echoes of the past do call,
But I won't let them make me fall.
In the stillness, I am reborn,
From ashes of the love once worn.

Tomorrow's dawn will bring new grace,
As I embrace this brighter space.
The art of letting go, I claim,
Transforming loss to wild acclaim.

With every tear, a seed takes root,
In fertile ground, my spirit shoots.
I rise above the weight of woe,
In the pure art of letting go.

Splintered Paths

Two roads diverge in evening light,
Both beckon softly in their plight.
Each direction whispers a tale,
Of dreams and hopes, or fear to fail.

The left is lined with shadows deep,
And secrets hidden, buried, steep.
The right, it glimmers with bright stars,
Promising peace, though still with scars.

I stand and ponder, heart in hand,
Which path will lead to promised land?
The mind delights in twisted turns,
Where every choice, a lesson learns.

With every step, the echoes wane,
The songs of choice, a haunting strain.
Yet in this maze, I carve my way,
Each splintered path, a new display.

So here I wander, brave and bold,
Embracing stories yet untold.
For life's a journey, wild and vast,
I dance upon the paths I've passed.

Dreams in Dissonance

In shadows where confusion stirs,
Lies a melody that whirs.
A symphony of hopes undone,
In tangled notes, we come unspun.

Chasing visions that slip away,
Like grains of sand at break of day.
A dissonance that fills the night,
Where dreams collide, yet seek the light.

Voices linger, faint and low,
Unwritten stories yet to grow.
Each heartbeat echoes lost refrain,
The bittersweet of love and pain.

Yet in the chaos, beauty glows,
A spark of joy that softly flows.
From discord, harmony may rise,
As we awaken with new eyes.

So here I stand, with open heart,
Embracing every fractured part.
For dreams in dissonance can sing,
A symphony of everything.

Silent Farewells

A glance exchanged, a fleeting breath,
In silence wrapped, we dance with death.
Each moment lingers, tastes of sweet,
A heavy heart in quiet beat.

No grand goodbyes, just whispered sighs,
As shadows deepen, time complies.
The weight of words hangs in the air,
Yet in this stillness, we both care.

With every step, a bond unwinds,
The threads of love, the ties that bind.
In quiet grace, we turn away,
Holding the echoes of yesterday.

Beneath the stars, where memories dwell,
We cast our dreams, the tales to tell.
Silent farewells, the dance of fate,
In every heartbeat, love awaits.

And though we part, our souls remain,
In whispered winds, in gentle rain.
For silent farewells, while bittersweet,
Are seeds of love that must repeat.

Chasing Fractured Dreams

In midnight's glow we chase the light,
Fragments of hope, a fleeting sight.
Shadows whisper soft and low,
Distant echoes from long ago.

Through shattered glass we seek to find,
The pieces left, the ties that bind.
Every heartbeat, a silent scream,
In the silence, we chase our dream.

With weary eyes and heavy hearts,
Navigating through the broken parts.
Yet in the ruins, we dare to stand,
Crafting futures with our hands.

The weight of doubts, a burdened past,
Yet we hold on, our spirits steadfast.
With each step through twilight's seam,
We rise again, chasing the dream.

Though storms may come and shadows loom,
We'll find our way through the thickest gloom.
In each fracture, a new light beams,
Together we'll mend our fractured dreams.

The Unraveling of Us

Tangled threads in twilight's glow,
Faded memories start to show.
Whispers quiet, hearts out of tune,
Once bright stars beneath the moon.

Each conversation, a fragile thread,
Words in silence, things left unsaid.
Once close kin, now drifting apart,
Unraveling seams of a broken heart.

The laughter shared, now echoes faint,
Brushstrokes of love turning to paint.
Fragments falling like autumn leaves,
As we navigate all our beliefs.

Yet in the twilight, hope may persist,
To rekindle the bond that we've missed.
Though time moves on and shadows blend,
Can we find our way and mend?

In the fabric of life we find our way,
We still believe in brighter days.
Through the unraveling, let's redefine,
The strength in us, a bond divine.

Pieces of the Unstoppable

In the fragments of what we've been,
Strength emerges from deep within.
Unyielding spirit, fierce and bright,
We'll rise together, ready for flight.

Each scar and bruise tells a tale,
Of battles fought, where we won't fail.
With every step, our resolve will grow,
Together we forge, together we flow.

Never broken, just rearranged,
In the chaos, we're uncontained.
With fierce hearts, we will reclaim,
The pieces of our endless flame.

Through storms we've weathered, we stand as one,
Chasing horizons, we won't be done.
In unity, we shatter the cage,
Unstoppable dreams take center stage.

In every heartbeat, a promise made,
In each challenge, our fears will fade.
Rising up, our spirits collide,
In pieces we find the unstoppable tide.

Remnants of Our Story

Amid the ruins, echoes remain,
Traces of laughter, hints of pain.
Pages crumpled, stories untold,
In every whisper, memories unfold.

The chapters blend, a tapestry spun,
With threads of twilight, they weave as one.
Silent tales in the softest light,
Remnants of what felt so right.

Footprints linger in paths we've crossed,
Though moments fade, we know the cost.
In every heartbeat, a lesson learned,
From every fire, a passion burned.

Though time may shift, and seasons change,
Our story remains, though it feels strange.
With ink of love, we write anew,
In remnants, there's strength to pursue.

Together we stand, hand in hand,
In the echoes of a promise planned.
Remnants of us, forever glow bright,
In the fabric of love, we find our light.

Time's Tattered Map

Beneath the stars, a path unfolds,
Each wrinkle tells a tale of old.
The hands of time, they stretch and bend,
Reminders of journeys that never end.

Through forests thick and mountains wide,
Lost in the echoes where dreams reside.
A compass cracked, yet still it strives,
To guide the heart where hope survives.

Footprints fade in shifting sand,
Yet memories of laughter still firmly stand.
With every turn, the past ignites,
In the soft glow of fading lights.

Maps drawn in ink, now blurred and stark,
Charting the realm of dreams that spark.
Worn edges whisper of wishes near,
As time reveals what we hold dear.

The journey winds, both near and far,
With every landmark, a guiding star.
We chase the moments that slip away,
In the dance of night and break of day.

Reflections in the Dark

In shadows deep, where whispers weave,
Silent thoughts, hard to believe.
The mirror shows a face unknown,
A heart that yearns to find its own.

Fragments lost in twilight's glow,
Haunting echoes of what we know.
Eyes like windows to hidden fears,
Telling tales of silent tears.

Beneath the stars, secrets ignite,
Casting dreams into the night.
Each flicker brings a moment's grace,
As we uncover our sacred space.

Caught in the web of fate's design,
Fleeting glimpses, threads intertwine.
In the dark, we find our light,
Guiding hearts through endless night.

In reflections faced, we stand so tall,
Together we rise, together we fall.
Through every shadow, we shall embark,
Embracing love that ignites the dark.

The Weight of Absence

An empty chair where laughter played,
Echoes linger in the shade.
Time drags slow, a heavy sigh,
In every heartbeat, a soft goodbye.

Memories dance in quiet rooms,
Faint applause for lost blooms.
A whisper fills the space once shared,
Echoing love, forever stared.

Each moment passed, a lingering ache,
Faces fade, but souls won't break.
In photographs, the smiles remain,
But in our hearts, we bear the pain.

The sun sets low, shadows creep,
In absence, the heart must keep.
Echoes of laughter, bittersweet,
In silence, we find where we meet.

Yet hope like blooms will rise anew,
Through gentle tears, shades of blue.
For love transcends the darkest night,
Transforming absence into light.

Shadows of Longing

In twilight's grasp, the shadows play,
Whispers of dreams that fade away.
A soft caress of fleeting time,
Yearning hearts in perfect rhyme.

Silent wishes drip like rain,
Mingling joy with echoing pain.
In the quiet, desires unfold,
In every story that needs retold.

Underneath the moon's soft glow,
Lovesick souls begin to grow.
Shadows linger, stretching long,
As we chase where we belong.

Each breath carries the weight of hope,
In the dark, we learn to cope.
The pull of dreams, both far and near,
Guiding us through what we fear.

With every heartbeat, longing coaxes,
Painting love in subtle strokes.
In shadows of twilight's embrace,
We find our truth in this sacred space.

The Last Melody

Whispers in the twilight glow,
An echo of a time we know.
Fingers dance on strings so light,
A melody that fades from sight.

Harmonies of dreams once spun,
Notes unraveled, one by one.
In the silence, memories tread,
A symphony of words unsaid.

Final chords in soft refrain,
Lingering like a gentle pain.
In the evening's cool embrace,
The last melody finds its place.

Songs of laughter, tears of years,
A tribute to our hopes and fears.
As shadows fall, the music sleeps,
In our hearts, the longing keeps.

So let the silence take its throne,
For in the quiet, we're not alone.
The last melody may depart,
But it forever lives in heart.

Dust Beneath the Stars

Footsteps linger on soft ground,
Stories lost but still profound.
Beneath the heavens' endless gaze,
Dust whispers of forgotten days.

Dreams entwined in cosmic tales,
As night winds weave through ancient trails.
Each grain a memory, softly spun,
Remnants of the lives once run.

Galaxies twinkle with silent grace,
Reflecting all we cannot trace.
In the vastness, we seek to find,
The connection that binds humankind.

Time may scatter, but love remains,
Echoes of laughter mixed with pains.
In the shadows of the firmament,
Dust beneath speaks of what we meant.

Breathe in the starlit, sacred fume,
The universe holds all our gloom.
Yet through the darkness, light will seep,
In the dust, our secrets keep.

Heartbeats Apart

Two souls carved from the same stone,
Drifting where the wild winds moan.
Every heartbeat, a silent plea,
Echoes of what's meant to be.

In the distance, a whisper grows,
Love's soft murmur, no one knows.
Bound by threads unseen and rare,
In the silence, we lay bare.

Miles may stretch, but we remain,
Tethered tight through joy and pain.
With every ache, each pulse ignites,
Reaching through the lonely nights.

Fingers brush on dreams once shared,
In the quiet, hearts have dared.
Though apart, we hold the spark,
It lights the path through the dark.

So let the world spin on its way,
For love will dawn with each new day.
In the rhythm, we'll find our start,
Together still, though far apart.

The Chorus of Lost Roads

Winding paths in dusky shade,
Memories of the choices made.
Each turn a whisper, soft yet clear,
As echoes of the past draw near.

Footsteps trace forgotten trails,
Love and loss in haunting tales.
A chorus sings of roads not taken,
In every note, our hearts awaken.

Stars align to guide our way,
Through the night, the map will sway.
In the dark, the spirit roams,
For every path leads us back home.

Songs of sorrow, hymns of grace,
As laughter lingers in this space.
For in the dance of fate, we find,
The roads we walk, forever bind.

So let the chorus rise and swell,
In every story, there's a spell.
Lost roads may fade, yet still they glow,
In the heart's embrace, they softly flow.

The Day the Colors Dimmed

The sky was gray, the sun withdrew,
Whispers of light began to fade.
Once vibrant hues turned dull and blue,
Memories lost in a heavy shade.

The flowers wilted, their smiles turned,
What once was bright, now draped in gloom.
Laughter faded, and silence churned,
Leaving echoes in every room.

Time moved on, yet shadows stayed,
A canvas marred by sorrow's hand.
Beauty dimmed, the dreams delayed,
As if the world could not withstand.

Through every tear, a lesson learned,
That colors shift with every sigh.
Yet in the dusk, hope still burned,
Awaiting dawn in the vast sky.

But through the dark, a light will break,
And paint anew the canvas wide.
For even when the heart may ache,
Resilience blooms where love did bide.

Tides of Forgetting

Waves roll in, a soft caress,
Memories sway like ships at sea.
Time pulls back, they drift, no less,
Into the depths of what will be.

Each tide retreats, a tale erased,
The shorelines shift beneath our feet.
What once was clear now lies misplaced,
The echoes of love, bittersweet.

Seagulls call, their cries remain,
While whispers fade in the salty air.
Beneath the waves, joy and pain,
Merge to create a dream we share.

Footprints lost in the shifting sand,
Each grain a moment slipping through.
Yet in our hearts, we understand,
That tides return with memories new.

So let the waves wash over us,
And learn to let the past be free.
In waves of time, we find a trust,
For all that fades, is part of me.

Ghosts of Affection

In every room, they leave their trace,
Fleeting shadows whisper soft goodbyes.
Warmth lingers still in empty space,
Memories dance like flickering lies.

Familiar laughter clings like lace,
Echoes hanging in the midnight air.
Lingering scents time can't erase,
Reminders of love's gentle care.

Moments trapped in photographs,
Frozen smiles that time won't claim.
Yet in stillness, a haunting laugh,
Ghosts of affection speak our name.

We carry them through every night,
Their love a blanket, warm and wide.
In the shadows, they hold us tight,
Reminding us of the joy inside.

So let us cherish what remains,
In whispered secrets brought to light.
These ghosts transform our earthly pains,
Into stars that shine throughout the night.

Shadows of Our Togetherness

Beneath the trees, we carved our names,
In bark that tells stories of our play.
The sunlight danced, in playful games,
As shadows wrapped us in their sway.

Each moment shared, a tender glance,
In laughter, in silence, we found grace.
The world was ours, a sweet romance,
With shadows drawing close, embracing space.

As seasons changed, our bonds did bend,
Still in the twilight, a light would share.
In every word, we found a friend,
With every shadow, a loving stare.

Through storms and skies, we stood as one,
Our silhouettes framed against the night.
In shadows deep, our hearts have spun,
Creating warmth, our guiding light.

And as we journey, hand in hand,
May shadows weave in love's embrace.
For in togetherness, we stand,
Creating memories, time can't erase.

Jigsaw of Memories

Fragments of laughter, scattered wide,
Echoes linger where dreams collide.
Pieces of time, both lost and found,
In the heart's puzzle, they spin around.

Faded photographs tangled in light,
Each moment treasured, held so tight.
Whispers of joy in the autumn's air,
Jigsaw of memories, everywhere.

Steps on the path, now overgrown,
Tracing the lines, the seeds we've sown.
Colors of yesterdays bleed in the dawn,
A mosaic of hopes, gently drawn.

Voices of friends who drifted away,
Echo in silence, from day to day.
Lost in the shuffle, a sweet refrain,
A jigsaw of memories, joy and pain.

Yet in the fragments, a light still shines,
Guiding the heart through tangled designs.
With every piece, a story unfolds,
In the jigsaw of memories, love retold.

Every Unsaid Word

In the silence, truth does weigh,
Every unsaid word finds its way.
Heavy with meaning, like shadows cast,
Lingering softly, ties to the past.

Thoughts left unspoken, ache in the breeze,
Bound in the silence, hearts seize with ease.
Moments tick by, feel the tension rise,
In the absence of sound, love softly cries.

Words on the tip, never dare flee,
Holding on tightly, lost in the sea.
Echoes of voices echo through night,
Every unsaid word yearns for the light.

Beneath the surface, emotions collide,
Every unsaid word, a secret confide.
With time's gentle grace, let shadows disperse,
Transforming our silence into a verse.

For in the unspoken, promise resides,
In the stillness, where feeling abides.
Every unsaid word, a story to weave,
In the tapestry of love, we believe.

Pieces on the Floor

Scattered like dreams that slip from our hands,
Pieces on the floor, where silence stands.
Fractured reflections, bright yet torn,
Stories forgotten, bruised and worn.

Shattered glass echoes with every fall,
A symphony of whispers, a haunting call.
Each shard a memory, sharp and clear,
Pieces on the floor, we hold so dear.

In the chaos, a beauty emerges,
From the fragments, our spirit surges.
Collecting the remnants of laughter and light,
Piecing together what's lost to the night.

Time's tender fingers, they mend and restore,
Transforming our pain into something more.
With courage we rise, though the world may roar,
Finding our strength in pieces on the floor.

With patience we build on this fractured site,
A mosaic of dreams, shifting through night.
Together we gather, hearts evermore,
Finding our wholeness in pieces on the floor.

Torn Between Tomorrows

Caught in the web of uncertain skies,
Torn between tomorrows, where promise lies.
Paths diverging in the soft morning glow,
In the choices we make, our dreams ebb and flow.

A glimpse of the future, a fleeting sight,
Whispers of hope in the fading light.
Choices unraveled, oh, where do we start?
Torn between tomorrows, following the heart.

Dancing on edges of fate's gentle hand,
Lost in the moments we struggle to stand.
Yet in the balance, a magic does brew,
Torn between tomorrows, discovering new.

With each whispered chance, a road to explore,
Awaiting the dawn behind every door.
As we wander through this delicate maze,
Torn between tomorrows, in wonder we gaze.

And in this journey, our spirits will soar,
Embracing the unknown, forevermore.
For even in shadows, the light we'll borrow,
In the dance of today, we'll mend our tomorrows.

In the Wake of Love's Loss

In shadows cast by love's retreat,
Memories linger, bittersweet.
Echoes haunt the quiet night,
A heart once whole, now lost from sight.

Tears like raindrops, softly flow,
Each one tells the tale of woe.
A fleeting touch, a tender glance,
Left behind, a broken chance.

Days stretch long, the silence vast,
Ghosts of laughter from the past.
Fading whispers in the air,
Remind me how you used to care.

Nighttime comes with aching dreams,
Of love that frayed at the seams.
Yet in the dark, I still believe,
In love's loss, we can retrieve.

From ashes, one can rise anew,
Finding strength in shades of blue.
For every end brings forth a start,
In the wake, we heal the heart.

The Dimming Light

As twilight falls, the world grows still,
A hush descends, a gentle thrill.
The sun dips low, horizon's grace,
A fading warmth, a soft embrace.

Whispers of dusk paint skies in gray,
Chasing the vibrant hues away.
Stars peep forth, shy and bright,
Against the canvas of the night.

Shadows lengthen, secrets creep,
Slowly lulling all to sleep.
The moon ascends, a silvery sigh,
Bathing the earth as night draws nigh.

In this dimming, beauty found,
A tranquil peace, a soothing sound.
For in the dark, the heart can see,
The quiet light that sets it free.

Hope flickers soft, a tender beam,
A guiding star in the dreamer's dream.
Through the night, we take our flight,
Finding our way in the dimming light.

A Canvas of Solitude

In solitude, the colors blend,
With every stroke, new feelings send.
A canvas stretched, a heart exposed,
Where quiet thoughts are gently enclosed.

Brush in hand, I craft my muse,
A world of dreams, I softly choose.
Each hue a whisper, each line a sigh,
Captured moments that pass me by.

In the stillness, I find my voice,
Amidst the silence, I rejoice.
A palette rich with pain and grace,
Reflecting truths I can embrace.

The brush dances, a waltz so free,
Creating visions only I can see.
In this solitude, I hold my fate,
An artful life where I create.

Each stroke a lesson, a step alone,
In this quiet space, I find my home.
For within this canvas, vast and wide,
I cherish the beauty I cannot hide.

Whispers Beneath the Stars

Under the blanket of the night,
Stars are stitched, a tapestry bright.
In whispers soft, the cosmos breathe,
Tales of wonder that hearts believe.

Moonlight dances on the sea,
Caressing waves, so wild and free.
In shadows cast by silver beams,
We share our hopes, our deepest dreams.

Each twinkling light, a story told,
Of love lost and of hearts bold.
Beneath the sky, we find our peace,
In celestial songs that never cease.

Time stands still, a gentle sigh,
As we gaze deep into the sky.
The universe, a boundless guide,
Whispers love that will abide.

In this moment, hearts entwined,
Holding dreams, our souls aligned.
Beneath the stars, forever ours,
Lost in the magic, count the stars.

The Weight of Unsaid Goodbyes

Words unspoken linger near,
Heavy hearts hold back the tear.
Promises fade in quiet night,
Dreams of closure out of sight.

Echoes of laughter fill the void,
Moments cherished, never destroyed.
Time stands still, the hourglass waits,
In silence, love contemplates.

Hope remains in shadows cast,
Yet knowing well this too shall pass.
Yet in the heart, a void will stay,
The weight of all we couldn't say.

Each glance shared, a word unsaid,
In the silence, paths we tread.
Memories etched in dimmest light,
Haunt the stars that fill the night.

In the end, we walk away,
With a burden none can say.
Finding strength in whispered sighs,
As we bear the unsaid goodbyes.

Hearts in Limbo

In the midst of what's unsure,
Hearts dance lightly, yet endure.
Holding on while letting go,
In the stillness, feelings flow.

Eyes that meet but never stay,
Words unmeant, left to decay.
Flickers of hope, whispers faint,
Painting dreams where love could paint.

Time hangs heavy, uncertain thread,
Lingering thoughts that won't be fed.
In this limbo, joy and strife,
Hearts seek meaning, seek to thrive.

Footsteps echo, paths unclear,
Yet we walk with nothing near.
In the shadows of the mind,
Hearts in limbo, love confined.

Finding solace in the pause,
Trusting fate without a cause.
In between the rise and fall,
Hearts in limbo, we hear the call.

A Symphony of Solitude

In empty rooms, the silence sings,
A melody of fragile things.
Echoes dance on walls so bare,
A symphony of quiet air.

Each note a whisper, soft and low,
Filling spaces where shadows grow.
In solitude, I find my grace,
A rhythm penned in this lost place.

Stars above in twilight's glow,
Chart the path where loners go.
In this vastness, I embrace,
The symphony of time and space.

Notes of longing weave through night,
Harmony born from absence's plight.
In stillness, hearts become aligned,
A symphony of souls confined.

Though alone, I'm not apart,
For in solitude, I find my heart.
With every pause, with every breath,
A symphony that conquers death.

Moments Now Adrift

Time escapes like grains of sand,
Moments slip through open hands.
In the tide of life, we float,
Drifting dreams on a lonely boat.

Waves of memory come and go,
Carrying whispers, soft and slow.
In this journey, lost we seem,
Chasing echoes of a dream.

Horizons blur, the shoreline fades,
In the twilight, light invades.
Each moment holds a fleeting grace,
Yet we wander, lost in space.

Stars above, our guiding light,
Navigate through the endless night.
In the depths of ocean's drift,
Moments weave a precious gift.

Letting go, embracing tides,
In the flow, our heart resides.
In the currents, we are free,
Moments now adrift at sea.

The Bitter End

In shadows cast by fading light,
A tale unwinds, a sorrowed plight.
Promises whispered, now forlorn,
The weight of love, forever worn.

Echoes linger in the dusk,
Words unspoken, bittersweet husk.
Memories dance in twilight's hue,
A heart once bold, now subdued.

Time drips slowly, like molten gold,
Stories of warmth, now cold.
Once vibrant dreams, now threadbare,
In the silence, only despair.

The clock counts down with heavy sighs,
Where joy once bloomed, now only cries.
The final act, curtains drawn tight,
Endings fade into the night.

Yet in this loss, a lesson learned,
For every fire, the heart has burned.
From ashes rise, new paths to tread,
In the bitter end, life is fed.

Dust on the Raft

Beneath the sun, the river flows,
A raft of dreams, where silence grows.
Dust collects on worn-out seams,
Forgotten hopes, abandoned schemes.

The gentle sway, a lullaby,
Nature's breath beneath the sky.
Ripples dance, a fleeting grace,
In stillness lies a sacred space.

Old tales whispered on the breeze,
Each grain of dust, a memory seized.
Worn hands grasping at the past,
Moments cherished, fading fast.

The horizon stretches, calling far,
Guiding hearts like a distant star.
Anchored dreams on water's edge,
With every wave, we walk the ledge.

But in the dusk, hope's ember glows,
The stream of life forever flows.
Dust may settle, but hearts remain,
In each breath, we find the gain.

Distant Harmonies

In the stillness, voices blend,
Echoes of hope, messages send.
Strains of laughter, threads of song,
Binding souls where we belong.

Through twilight's veil, the music swells,
Carried forth by distant bells.
A melody, soft and profound,
Weaving stories all around.

Beneath the stars, we gather near,
Swaying gently, casting fear.
In harmony, hearts intertwine,
Redeeming moments, pure and divine.

Yet shadows lurk just out of sight,
Dissonance born of the night.
But as the dawn brings forth the day,
Unity shines, showing the way.

So let the music guide our feet,
In distant harmonies, we meet.
Each note a promise, sweetly sung,
Together, forever, ever young.

Waves of Solitude

A lonely shore, the ocean sighs,
Waves crash gently, time flies.
In solitude, the heart does roam,
Seeking peace, a distant home.

Salt kisses skin, the breeze whispers,
In each wave's crash, a heart's luster.
With every pulse, a tale unfolds,
Of silent journeys, brave and bold.

Drifting thoughts on the tide's embrace,
As moonlight dances on the face.
Solitude speaks in whispers low,
A sacred bond, only we know.

Yet through the dark, the stars will shine,
Guiding us, though paths entwine.
In the night, a quiet cheer,
For in this solitude, love is near.

So let the waves wash dreams ashore,
With every ebb, we hope for more.
In solitude's grace, hearts align,
In quiet moments, life is divine.

Horizon of Haze

Veils of gray stretch wide and far,
Whispers dance beneath the stars.
Mountains fade in soft embrace,
Time retreats, a fleeting trace.

Mist that cloaks the waking morn,
Secrets lost, yet dreams are born.
A world dissolved in colors pale,
Guiding hearts through every trial.

Silhouettes upon the shore,
Echoes linger, evermore.
Tidal waves of silent sighs,
Horizon gasps as daylight flies.

Beyond the clouds, a spark ignites,
Hope emerges, brave as night.
In the depths of endless gray,
The horizon calls, a new day.

Light cascades on muted ground,
In the haze, lost dreams are found.
Each breath fills the quiet space,
A promise waits, a warm embrace.

Unlatched Doors

Keys lie scattered on the floor,
Echoes linger by the door.
Fingers trace the wood's fine grain,
Memories dance through joy and pain.

Behind each door, a story weaves,
Whispers held in soft, woven leaves.
Light slips through the cracks and seams,
Awakening our buried dreams.

Unlatched, they beckon with a sigh,
Promises of moments gone by.
A gentle pull, the past returns,
In every heart, a fire burns.

Time invites us to explore,
Every passage an open door.
With every step, we find our way,
Into the night, into the day.

Each door reveals a fragile hope,
A chance to heal, a place to cope.
Brave the shadows, embrace the light,
In the silence, dreams take flight.

Echoes of a Shattered Heart

Fragments scattered on the floor,
Each piece whispers, evermore.
Siren songs of love once true,
Haunt the hallways, lingering view.

Lost in shadows of what was,
Yearning fades without a cause.
Echoes dance in empty space,
Time slows down, a bittersweet race.

Heartbeats sync with distant drums,
A melody of love succumbs.
Every sigh a memory flows,
In the silence, sorrow grows.

Light may flicker, yet it shines,
Illuminating broken lines.
Each wound carries strength anew,
Resilience born from pain we knew.

Glimmers rise from deep despair,
A spark igniting hope laid bare.
In each echo, lessons weave,
From shattered hearts, we learn to breathe.

Fragments of Yesterday

Scattered pieces of the past,
Moments fleeting, shadows cast.
Memories fade like autumn leaves,
Whispers carried on the breeze.

Fragments glimmer in the night,
Silent stories take their flight.
Where laughter danced, now echoes dwell,
In every heart, a secret spell.

Time slips through our fragile hands,
Dreams dissolve like shifting sands.
Yet in the stillness, we can hear,
The cadence of those we hold dear.

Every piece a tale to tell,
Woven moments where we fell.
In our hearts, they find their place,
Fragments held in warm embrace.

Tomorrow waits with open arms,
A chance to weave new, vibrant charms.
Yet as we walk, we carry near,
Fragments of yesterday, so clear.

The Dusk of Us

The sun dips low, a golden hue,
Shadows stretch, as night breaks through.
Whispers linger on the fading light,
Memories dance in the soft twilight.

Promises made in the twilight glow,
Threads of silver, a gentle flow.
Familiar paths we used to roam,
In dusk's embrace, we find our home.

Echoes of laughter, now bittersweet,
Footsteps falter on memories' sheet.
Underneath this fading sky,
We cherish moments, yet wonder why.

Hearts entwined in the coming dark,
The night reveals a hidden spark.
What once was bright now softly glows,
In the dusk of us, the fervor slows.

A world transformed where dreams reside,
In our silence, the truth won't hide.
Together we linger, the past in view,
The dusk of us, a love so true.

Silent Reverberations

In the quiet corners, secrets hide,
Ripples of silence, like the ocean's tide.
Echoes of thoughts drift through the air,
In empty spaces, we're still aware.

Whispers linger where words can't go,
In the silence, emotions flow.
Heartbeats sync in a gentle refrain,
Silent reverberations, joy and pain.

The moonlit night holds such calm,
A soothing balm, nature's psalm.
Under the stars, our fears take flight,
In silent moments, we find the light.

Time hangs still in a breath held long,
In the quiet, we find our song.
A melody sweet, soft as a sigh,
Silent reverberations, you and I.

When voices fade into the night,
The silence cradles our shared light.
In the echoes, love's pulse thrives,
Silent reverberations, where hope arrives.

The Calm in Our Chaos

In the storm's eye, we find our peace,
A gentle harbor that will not cease.
Waves may crash, and thunder may roll,
Yet in our hearts, we feel the whole.

Through tangled paths, we navigate,
Hand in hand, we won't hesitate.
Chaos swirls in vivid display,
Yet love's embrace guides us each day.

With every trial, our bond grows strong,
In discord's dance, we find the song.
Amidst the noise, our whispers blend,
In the calm, our spirits mend.

We breathe as one, a steady beat,
In life's chaos, we find our seat.
Hearts colliding in the wild night,
Together we stand, ready to fight.

Let the world storm, let the winds blow,
In our chaos, there's much to sow.
With every challenge, we rise anew,
The calm in our chaos, me and you.

Unspoken Changes

In the stillness, we sense the shift,
Unseen currents, a subtle gift.
Words unspoken hang in the air,
In quiet glances, we lay bare.

Leaves fall softly, a gentle sign,
Time moves onward, like aged wine.
Moments whisper secrets untold,
In hearts once bright, now quietly bold.

We shape our paths with silent grace,
Change draws near to our warm embrace.
In the spaces where silence grows,
Unspoken changes, the heart knows.

What was familiar now feels so strange,
Yet growth demands its own exchange.
In every silence, a truth reveals,
Unspoken changes, the heart's appeals.

Together we journey, hand in hand,
Through the unknown, we firmly stand.
Embracing shifts as seasons wane,
In unspoken changes, love remains.

Glimmering Remnants

In shadows long and whispers low,
The night reveals a softened glow.
Faint memories dance in twilight's hand,
Glimmers of dreams, like grains of sand.

Lost treasures hide in heart's embrace,
Eclipsed by time, yet find their place.
Time's canvas holds their timeless grace,
A gentle touch, a warm trace.

Starlit paths weave through the dark,
Guiding hearts with a luminous spark.
In every laugh, in every sigh,
Glimmers of love can never die.

Echoes of laughter fill the air,
Each moment shared, a silent prayer.
In glimmering remnants, we find our way,
A tapestry colored by yesterday.

So hold these glimmers close and tight,
For they will guide you through the night.
In fleeting time, they softly hum,
Glimmering remnants of what we've become.

Fading Footprints

Along the shore where waves retreat,
Fading footprints mark the heat.
A dance of souls in fleeting sand,
Memories left by love's own hand.

With every tide that pulls away,
The past dissolves, but here we stay.
Worn paths tell tales of joy and pain,
In whispered winds, echoes remain.

Like shadows cast from setting sun,
Life's journey tells of battles won.
Yet as the light begins to fade,
There lies a beauty unafraid.

Each step we take, a story told,
In fading footprints, dreams unfold.
Though time may wash them from our sight,
Their spirit lingers, pure and bright.

So cherish each and every stride,
For in our hearts, those marks abide.
In fading footprints, love endures,
A silent promise that reassures.

The Space Between Us

In silence thick, where whispers pause,
Lies a distance that gently draws.
A heartbeat shared, yet worlds apart,
The space between us, a tender art.

Eyes that meet, yet words can't find,
In fleeting glances, souls aligned.
A breath away, though miles extend,
In the space between, love can mend.

Time stretches thin, like threads of gold,
Binding warmth in stories bold.
Every sigh holds a universe,
The space between us, a silent verse.

In dreams we dance, in rhythms sweet,
The space between, where pulses beat.
Though distances may cloud our sight,
Love fills the void, igniting light.

So let us cherish the quiet space,
That carries us in its warm embrace.
For in this space, we learn to trust,
The distance binds, a sacred must.

Broken Halos

In twilight's glow, where shadows blend,
Broken halos bend and mend.
Fractured light upon the ground,
A beauty sought, yet rarely found.

With whispered dreams and hopes that soar,
These broken halos yearn for more.
In every flaw, a story lies,
Reflections caught in fractured skies.

Stars will flicker, then fade away,
Yet in their glow, we find our way.
Each fragment tells of battles fought,
In glowing remnants, lessons taught.

So lift your eyes; let shadows play,
In broken halos, find your way.
For in the cracks, there's light that beams,
A tribute to our ancient dreams.

Embrace the scars, let laughter flow,
For broken halos teach us glow.
In every gap, in every break,
There lies a light that we can make.

The Não of Yesterday

In shadows where dreams softly fade,
The weight of what was left unmade.
Whispers linger like ghosts in the air,
Holding onto moments we could not share.

Each choice a path, a fork in the road,
Echoes telling tales, heavy like a load.
The não of yesterday haunts my mind,
As I seek the answers I'm yet to find.

Time dances lightly, but scars remain,
Reminders of love wrapped in pain.
Fragments of laughter, echoes of tears,
Tracing the outlines of all my fears.

Yet in the stillness, a flicker of hope,
Glimmers of light on an unsteady slope.
The não is a lesson, not just a chain,
Finding strength in the heartache and strain.

With every sunrise, a chance to reclaim,
The missed opportunities lost in the flame.
Step by step, I learn to forgive,
In the não of yesterday, I choose to live.

Wounds Beneath the Surface

Invisible battles fought every day,
Wounds that are hidden, kept far away.
Beneath the calm, a tempest brews,
Each heartbeat a whisper of silent blues.

Masks of the cheerful, laughter that rings,
Covering stories that pain often brings.
In the deepest trenches, shadows reside,
Longing for solace, for someone to guide.

Beneath the surface, a river of tears,
Flowing unchecked, fed by fears.
Yet in that darkness, a spark may ignite,
Strength that emerges in the dead of night.

Healing requires a tender embrace,
Learning to trust and find a safe place.
Wounds may linger, but hope is alive,
The journey to wholeness is where we thrive.

Through every scar, a story unfolds,
Bravery shines where the heart is bold.
Wounds beneath the surface remind me to see,
The beauty in strength and the power to be.

When Silence Speaks

In the quiet corners where shadows play,
Words become echoes, drifting away.
The stillness around holds secrets unsaid,
When silence speaks, it fills up my head.

Hands intertwined, no need for a sound,
In the hush of the moment, love can be found.
Gazes that linger, a language of eyes,
In silence, the heart learns to rise.

A breath held tight, anticipation sweet,
In the pause, the world feels complete.
When silence speaks, all fears seem to melt,
In the tender embrace, true feelings are felt.

Words may escape, lost in the breeze,
Yet silence can comfort, can soothe and please.
Through unspoken thoughts, deep truths align,
When silence speaks, our souls intertwine.

In a world so loud, let the quiet remain,
For when silence speaks, we have much to gain.
In the gentle hush, let love be our guide,
For in that stillness, hearts open wide.

Distant Lullabies

Softly they drift on the wings of the night,
Distant lullabies, a gentle delight.
Carried by whispers that roam through the skies,
Melodies echo where passion lies.

Each note a story, a dream left to chase,
Painting the air with a timeless grace.
In shadows of moonlight, they find their way,
Distant lullabies at the end of the day.

Crickets serenade, nature joins in,
Harmony wraps like a silken skin.
With every heartbeat, a promise to keep,
In that soothing cadence, the world drifts to sleep.

Moments suspended, as time softly sways,
Distant lullabies leading hearts to rays.
A sweet invitation to dance with the stars,
With love in the silence, no matter how far.

Whispers and echoes will never depart,
Distant lullabies cradling the heart.
In the stillness and shadows, dreams intertwine,
In each tender note, the universe shines.

The Break Between Heartbeats

In shadows cast by whispered dreams,
A silence lingers, tearing seams.
The pulse of hope begins to fade,
In every breath, a choice is made.

Moments lost in fleeting time,
A chime that echoes, lost in rhyme.
Between the beats, our heartstrings fray,
The space between, a price to pay.

In distant echoes, voices blend,
A melody of loss, my friend.
Yet still we grasp at what we know,
Beyond the void, we ebb and flow.

The sigh of leaves in autumn's breeze,
A fading warmth, the heart's unease.
In every pause, a truth revealed,
The pain of love, the wound unhealed.

And so we dance, in twilight's glow,
With fractured chords, our sorrow's show.
But in the break, a hope remains,
A flicker bright, despite the chains.

Ghostwritten Goodbyes

On pages stained with sorrow's ink,
We write our tales, then pause and think.
Each word a weight, a heart unbound,
In every line, a loss is found.

Beneath the veil of whispered fears,
A symphony of silent tears.
The ink runs dry, our stories fade,
In every chapter, memories laid.

We script the lines of our decline,
As moments dance through tangled time.
In ghostly echoes, goodbye rings clear,
Yet in the heart, you linger near.

A tender touch, a fleeting glance,
The lost embrace of a cruel chance.
With every page, the end draws nigh,
In ghostwritten words, we learn to fly.

But love remains, a writing's art,
Forever etched within the heart.
In every ending, something starts,
A timeless bond that never departs.

The Map of Our Divergence

In scattered stars, we trace our ways,
A fading path through twilight haze.
Each choice a line upon the map,
A journey drawn with every gap.

Our footsteps speak in silent tones,
Through winding roads, we walk alone.
Yet in the distance, echoes call,
The whispers of a love that falls.

With every turn, new paths we roam,
In unfamiliar lands, we're home.
The map unfolds with every sigh,
In every tear, a silent why.

Countries crossed and borders breached,
Lessons learned and hearts were reached.
Yet still, within this vast expanse,
The hope remains for one last chance.

So let us chart the stars above,
And navigate the seas of love.
For even when our paths diverge,
In every heartbeat, still we merge.

A Bridge to Silence

Where words once flowed like rivers wide,
Now echoes linger, hearts divide.
A bridge now stands, both fragile, strong,
In silence, still, the souls belong.

Each whisper lost, a chance untouched,
Our voices hushed, emotions clutched.
Yet in the stillness, beauty grows,
A quiet strength that only knows.

Between the spans, an endless void,
Where laughter danced, now pain deployed.
Yet silence holds a sacred space,
In every pause, a hidden grace.

The bridge we built now sways with time,
Balancing love, the bitter, sweet rhyme.
Yet in each heartbeat, memories gleam,
A bridge to silence isn't what it seems.

So let us walk with open hearts,
Through whispered dreams where nothing parts.
For in the silence, love can thrive,
A bridge that keeps our souls alive.

Whispers of the Lost

In the moonlight's gentle haze,
Where shadows dance and play,
Voices echo from the past,
Whispers of the lost, they sway.

In secret groves, they linger still,
Beneath the ancient trees,
Tales of love and dreams unspilled,
Carried softly by the breeze.

Faint murmurs in the starlit night,
Call to hearts that yearn,
For every moment, every light,
That fate has made to burn.

Through the silence, time will weave,
A thread of longing bright,
Every sigh a chance to grieve,
Whispered hopes take flight.

In the fading twilight's grace,
Echoes fade yet resonate,
For in each heart lies a space,
Where whispers love and fate articulate.

The Abyss of Departure

At the edge where dark meets light,
The horizon starts to wane,
Steps into the void of night,
Fading hopes, a silent pain.

Glimmers of what once was bright,
Now drift like clouds of grey,
With every heartbeat, every flight,
Another piece slips away.

A distant call, a farewell sigh,
As moments turn to dust,
With every tear, a silent why,
A heart's betrayal of trust.

The path ahead is cold and stark,
With shadows looming near,
In the silence, there's a spark,
Offering solace for fear.

Embrace the void, let go the past,
For every ending, a start,
In the abyss, hold dreams steadfast,
And allow love's light to chart.

Paintings in Shadow

Brushstrokes of light and dark,
Crafting worlds of silent grace,
In every corner, a hidden spark,
Revealing dreams in shadowed space.

A canvas whispers tales untold,
Of loves lost and battles won,
Where colors blend, both brave and bold,
Beneath the gaze of the sun.

In the depths of vibrant hue,
Lies a heart both fierce and meek,
For every shade, a story new,
Each stroke a voice, profound yet sleek.

Through layers thick, emotions weave,
A tapestry of truth and pain,
In shadows deep, we still believe,
Art is where we find our gain.

So let the brush move free and wild,
Creating echoes of our soul,
In every line, the heart of a child,
Finding beauty that makes us whole.

Cinders of Our Flame

Once a blaze that brightly shone,
Now embers fade to ash,
In the quiet heart's deep bone,
Memories of a love gone crash.

Sparkling laughter, warm and sweet,
Now echoes in the void,
What once was whole, now feels incomplete,
By silence, hearts are toyed.

Cinders whisper of what was sweet,
In the shadow's fading glow,
Fragments of love still feel complete,
Yet reality's sharp blow.

Holding tightly to the past,
With every thought, we ignite,
Though the flames may not last,
The warmth still feels so right.

In the ashes, hope can rise,
Rekindle dreams from what remains,
For in the dark, the spirit flies,
And love's song still explains.

Ashes of What Once Shone

In the glow of faded light,
We search for whispers past.
Memories like embers bright,
Are shadows now cast.

Once a fire burned so high,
Now only smoke remains.
Dreams that soared, now float and sigh,
In quiet, lonely pains.

Tales of laughter, tales of joy,
Lost in the silent night.
What was once a cherished toy,
Now out of reach, out of sight.

Time has turned the vibrant hue,
To ashes soft and gray.
But in the heart, residue,
Of warmth that used to stay.

Yet in these ashes, sparks still gleam,
A flicker of what's true.
In the darkness, reignite a dream,
For there's life yet to pursue.

The Hourglass of Us

Time slips through our fingers quick,
   Like grains of sand at play.
Each moment a thrilling trick,
   In this dance we sway.

With every tick, a sigh escapes,
   Cascading whispers shared.
In the shape of our heartscapes,
   A bond forever bared.

The glass turns slow, then rushes fast,
   A puzzle made of now.
Echoing what once has passed,
   But in the how, the vow.

We chase the shade of daylight true,
   Through shadows long and wide.
In this hourglass meant for two,
   We find where dreams abide.

So let the sands of time be kind,
   Embracing what we feel.
For in this moment, hearts entwined,
   Our love's the truest seal.

Shadows Between the Lines

In the pages where we write,
A tale of hearts in flight.
Every word a soft caress,
In verses we confess.

Yet shadows linger, whisper low,
In corners, bits we know.
Not all tales come clear to light,
Some hidden fears take flight.

With ink of hopes and dreams we spill,
We draft what time will kill.
But in between the written space,
Are shadows we embrace.

Each line that draws us close and far,
Marks battles lost and scar.
In the silence, truths reside,
In shadows, we abide.

Yet still we pen this fragile song,
In echoes where we belong.
For between each word we find,
The beauty intertwined.

Tender Ruins

Among the rocks, the softest chill,
A heart once fierce now still.
In the ruins where we tread,
Lies love, not dead, but spread.

Tender whispers haunt the air,
Of moments we could share.
Echoes of a sweet embrace,
Once a loved, familiar place.

Vines and shadows wrap the stone,
In silence, we atone.
For dreams that cracked and fell apart,
But still reside within our heart.

Led by memories so divine,
We gather what is mine.
Amongst the fragments, still we find,
The threads of love that bind.

So let the tender ruins stand,
As testament, so grand.
For here where once the laughter bloomed,
We cultivate our groomed.

Love's Fading Palette

Once vibrant hues now dull and pale,
Memories linger, soft and frail.
Brushstrokes of laughter, shades of tears,
A canvas bearing silent fears.

Whispers of warmth in twilight's glow,
Fading colors, as soft winds blow.
Once bold expressions, now subdued,
Love's artistry, a changing mood.

Seasons shift, as time insists,
The brighter days, we can't resist.
Yet, in the quiet, beauty remains,
In every shadow, love's refrains.

Though colors blend in gentle sighs,
Tender glances, heartfelt lies.
As twilight deepens into night,
We hold on tight, despite the flight.

With every stroke, a tale unfolds,
Of whispered dreams and hands to hold.
Though love may fade, its essence stays,
Forever etched in life's array.

The Unspoken Rift

Between us lies a fragile seam,
A silence hanging like a dream.
Words unsaid, like ghosts they roam,
Haunting corners of our home.

Eyes avoid in whispered shame,
Yet hearts still beat, the same old game.
Moments shared, now laced with doubt,
Where love was once, there's only shout.

Bridges built and yet they break,
Trust dissolving, wills to shake.
Laughter now feels out of place,
As we dance in a divided space.

What was sacred, now feels raw,
Each glance tells tales of an unspoken flaw.
Yearning to mend, but fear resides,
In the deep where silence hides.

Clutched memories, we let them fade,
Inside the rift, where dreams wade.
Yet hope flickers, a distant light,
As we seek to make wrongs ignite.

In shadows deep, our hearts may ache,
To bridge the gap, for love's own sake.
A gentle whisper, a silent plea,
May heal the rift, set us free.

Threads of Yesterday

Woven tightly, moments stored,
In the fabric of time, we adored.
Colors vibrant, memories bright,
Tales unfolding in gentle light.

Threads of laughter, looms of tears,
Stitches binding all our years.
Softly woven, dreams interlace,
Each strand a story, time can't erase.

In each knot, a lesson learned,
In every turn, a heart that yearned.
A tapestry of joy and pain,
Threads of yesterday still remain.

The fabric fades but never frays,
In the quilt of life, love displays.
Stitched together through thick and thin,
A testament to where we've been.

Through every tear, we mend anew,
A legacy in every hue.
With every stitch, we weave our fate,
Threads of yesterday, love's estate.

In quiet moments, these threads we hold,
A cherished narrative to unfold.
Though time may pass, the ties remain,
In every heartbeat, love's refrain.

Quiet Goodbyes

In stillness dwells the parting breath,
A silent echo, a whispered death.
No grand exits, no raging storms,
Just quiet moments, where heart conforms.

A lingering glance, a final touch,
Words unspoken, that mean so much.
In soft goodbyes, we find our peace,
As love releases, we seek our lease.

Time stands still in this embrace,
Each heartbeat slows, a measured pace.
Memories flood as eyes grow wet,
In every pause, a love we set.

The door creaks open, shadows blend,
Yet in this silence, we ascend.
A journey shared, now diverging ways,
In quiet goodbyes, our hearts still blaze.

Through endless nights and somber days,
Life continues, though love sways.
In every moment, we'll find the grace,
To cherish those quiet goodbyes we face.

With gentle hope, we'll find our day,
In quiet goodbyes, love leads the way.
Through every tear, the heart will guide,
In whispered echoes, we bide, abide.

The Lament of Two Souls

In shadows deep, where silence weeps,
Two souls wander, through time's endless leaps.
With whispers faint, their spirits sigh,
Bound by love, yet forced to fly.

Stars above, a witness to their plight,
Yearning hearts, lost in the night.
Every tear, a tale untold,
In the chill, their warmth grows cold.

Fate's cruel hand, a bitter test,
Together apart, they long for rest.
Through fractured dreams, they seek the dawn,
But in the light, one soul is gone.

Time marches on, a ruthless beast,
Yet hope lingers, a faithful feast.
With every ache, their spirits blend,
A love unbroken, amidst the end.

In silent prayers, their voices merge,
Two souls entwined, a boundless surge.
Though paths diverge, their essence stays,
In every heart, their memory plays.

A Tapestry Torn

Threads once woven, vibrant and bright,
Now unravel, lost in the night.
Colors fade, and patterns fray,
A tapestry torn, drifted away.

Each stitch a story, rich and deep,
Now scattered dreams, no more to keep.
Silent echoes in every strand,
A fabric once held in gentle hand.

Memories flicker like candles low,
Guiding hands, now moving slow.
In shadows cast, the truth unfolds,
A quilt obscured, with tales untold.

Hearts entwined in the weave of fate,
Yet threads break, love resonates.
Through the tears, new patterns form,
In chaos, beauty begins to swarm.

Fragments linger in the loom of time,
A blend of sorrow, and love's sweet rhyme.
Though torn apart, the heart will mend,
A tapestry grows, through every end.

Fractured Bonds

In the stillness, silence grows,
Fractured bonds, where love once glows.
Promises linger, shadowed and worn,
In the light, the heart feels torn.

Once hand in hand, now lost in dreams,
Echoes of laughter fade at the seams.
Through quiet whispers, hopes collide,
Love's fragile thread, stretched far and wide.

Time drifts on, a gentle thief,
Stealing moments, causing grief.
Yet in the dark, a spark remains,
Hope navigates through all the pains.

Two souls adrift on separate seas,
With memories drifting on the breeze.
Yet shadows dance where light breaks through,
Fractured bonds can grow anew.

In the heart's depths, resilience stirs,
For every end, a path infers.
Through broken chains, love finds a way,
To heal the soul, and lead the sway.

Uncharted Echoes

Through valleys deep, where shadows creep,
Uncharted echoes in silence seep.
Whispers wander, soft as mist,
In the twilight, dreams persist.

Footsteps trace the path unknown,
In the heart, a thirst has grown.
Every sigh, a prayer sent high,
To chase the stars beyond the sky.

In the stillness, hope takes flight,
Carried forth on wings of night.
With every breath, the worlds collide,
In laughter shared, no need to hide.

In echoes soft, the past resounds,
Lost in time, where wisdom founds.
With open hearts, the journey starts,
Uncharted paths for wandering hearts.

Through valleys forged in love's embrace,
Eternal echoes find their place.
Together onward, side by side,
In uncharted realms, hearts will guide.

The Spaces Between Us

In silence we dwell, a chasm wide,
Words left unspoken, like waves that divide.
Hearts reaching out, yet drifting away,
In the spaces between, where shadows sway.

The stars may align in the night sky,
But distance remains, as we question why.
Moments once shared, now faint and unclear,
In the echo of whispers, we part with a tear.

Though paths may diverge, the bond lingers on,
In dreams we return, where hopes are reborn.
A flicker of light, in the darkness we find,
In the spaces between, our hearts intertwined.

Yet time marches forth, with its ceaseless demands,
We navigate storms, with invisible hands.
The love that once flourished, now tangled and fraught,
In the spaces between, we dwell on what's sought.

Will healing come forth, like spring after frost?
Or linger in shadows, in longing, at cost?
In the end, we'll discover, with courage anew,
That the spaces between can bring us to you.

Solitary Whispers

In a room filled with echoes, I sit all alone,
The shadows dance softly, their presence is known.
Silence envelops me, thick like a shroud,
In solitary whispers, I call to the crowd.

Thoughts drift like feathers, on a breeze full of dreams,
Where hope gently flickers, in sunlight it gleams.
Each sigh holds a secret, each breath tells a tale,
In the solitude's arms, they rise and they sail.

I listen for answers, in the stillness of night,
The moon casts reflections, with soft silver light.
In shadows I ponder, what memories hold,
In solitary whispers, the stories unfold.

The world spins around me, a whirlwind of sound,
Yet here in this moment, peace I have found.
A heart wrapped in silence, knows no need for the jest,
In solitary whispers, my spirit finds rest.

From the depths of the quiet, a voice starts to rise,
A gentle reminder, to open my eyes.
Though alone I may wander, my heart is not weak,
In the solitude's embrace, my soul learns to speak.

Threads Unraveled

A tapestry woven, in colors so bright,
Yet life pulls the threads, revealing its plight.
Frayed edges and knots, where stories collide,
In the threads unraveled, no truth left to hide.

Each moment a stitch, in the fabric of fate,
Time weaves its patterns, it's never too late.
We gather the remnants, and cherish our woes,
In the threads unraveled, our history grows.

The fabric may fray, and the colors may fade,
But in every loose strand, a memory made.
With hands that are weary, we lift up our loom,
In the threads unraveled, we craft through the gloom.

A quilt of past sorrows, patterns entwined,
In fragile connections, resilience we find.
Stitch by stitch onward, we create our design,
In the threads unraveled, our journeys align.

And though the threads tangle, and may not set straight,
Each twist brings us closer, we learn to create.
In the tapestry's heart, our truths interlace,
In the threads unraveled, we find our own grace.

Faded Reflections

In mirrors obscured, where memories lie,
Faded reflections whisper and sigh.
Time brushes softly, like dust o'er the glass,
In faded reflections, moments now pass.

Faces once vivid, now shadows of light,
Echoes of laughter, that fade into night.
Each glimmer of beauty feels distant, removed,
In faded reflections, the heart's truth is proved.

We search for the colors that painted our youth,
In sepia tones, we unravel the truth.
With hands reaching out, to catch what is lost,
In faded reflections, we bear all the cost.

But wisdom comes softly, through lines on our skin,
In each faded moment, new journeys begin.
The past does not vanish, it lingers, it calls,
In faded reflections, we rise from our falls.

So we cherish the echoes, the laughter, the tears,
In faded reflections, we conquer our fears.
The stories we carry, forever etched clear,
In faded reflections, we hold them quite near.

Fractured Echoes

In the depths of night, whispers call,
Each shadow dances, a lonely thrall.
Reflections murmur of times long past,
While memories flutter, too fragile to last.

A heartbeat echoes in broken dreams,
Carrying secrets on moonlit streams.
The world around hums a mournful song,
Yet in this silence, we still belong.

Cracked facades hold stories untold,
Fragments of love that the heart can't hold.
In every fissure, a tale unfolds,
Of laughter and sorrow, of warmth and cold.

Through shattered paths where shadows tread,
We search for light, where hope had fled.
Yet, even in fractures, beauty can shine,
In the echo of voices, eternally entwined.

So let us gather the pieces we find,
From the ruins of heart, we don't leave behind.
Together we stand, though worlds may bend,
In fractured echoes, we learn to mend.

Shattered Threads

Woven stories unravel at night,
With every pull, fading from sight.
Colors collide in chaotic grace,
As dreams slip through this fragile space.

Tangled in whispers of voices old,
Each strand carries wishes, brave and bold.
Yet silken knots can bind the heart,
In the fabric of life, we're torn apart.

Glimmers of joy in the fibers remain,
Stitches of laughter, and stitches of pain.
Through the shards of memories once we knew,
In the tapestry's weave, love always grew.

A needle dances, though hands may shake,
With every loop, we mend what breaks.
Together in threads, we find our way,
In shattered patterns, a new array.

So gather the pieces, hold them tight,
In the warmth of love, we find our light.
With every stitch, a story is spun,
In shattered threads, our lives are one.

The Weight of Silence

A heavy pause in a crowded space,
Unspoken words hang, a ghostly trace.
Each heartbeat echoes the thoughts we hide,
In the weight of silence, we bide our pride.

Glances linger, where words should dance,
Fractured moments, a fleeting chance.
The air thickens as hope fades away,
In silence's grasp, our fears hold sway.

Memories clamor for voices to dare,
Yet silence binds what we cannot share.
A gentle sigh floats between us two,
In the weight of silence, love must break through.

Shadows stretch long with a muted sigh,
Yet silence teaches us how to fly.
In the aching quiet, truths will collide,
In the weight of silence, we learn to confide.

So listen closely, my dear friend,
For silence speaks of the love we send.
Through the weight of all that is left unsaid,
In quietude, our hearts are fed.

Splintered Hearts

Once whole, now fractured beyond repair,
We weave through moments, lost in despair.
A jagged edge where love used to be,
In splintered hearts, we yearn to be free.

Cruel fate dealt blows, sharp and unkind,
Leaving us grasping for what we can't find.
Yet in the chaos, a flicker resides,
In splintered hearts, a flame abides.

Beneath the scars lies a strength untold,
Each piece a memory, cherished, bold.
In the depths of sorrow, resilience grows,
While splintered hearts learn how love glows.

Together we gather the shards on our way,
Creating a path where shadows may sway.
In the dance of night, we find our beat,
In splintered hearts, we are still complete.

So cherish each fragment, hold it dear,
For in every sliver, love draws near.
Through splintered hearts, we mend and thrive,
In our brokenness, we come alive.

Tethered No More

In shadows cast by aching dreams,
I find the strength to break the seams.
With every step, the chains do fall,
I rise above, I heed the call.

Where once I stood in silent fear,
Now courage blooms, my path is clear.
The ties that bound me to the ground,
Are shattered now, I make my sound.

No longer lost in someone else,
I claim the power that's myself.
With open heart and mind untied,
I fly away, I will not hide.

The past a whisper in my ear,
A distant echo, soon not near.
I soar above the boundless sea,
A spirit wild, forever free.

Tethered no more, I find my place,
In every star, in every space.
Embracing life with open arms,
The world awaits, with all its charms.

The Frost of Forgotten Affection

In winter's grasp, the silence sighs,
A love once warm, now cold like ice.
The memories dance on frosty air,
A ghost of joy, nothing to share.

Beneath the snow, what used to bloom,
Lies buried deep in frozen gloom.
Each whisper lost in winter's breath,
A tale of love now fraught with death.

The hearth so dim, the embers fade,
What once was light, now cast in shade.
I walk through rooms where laughter grew,
And search for signs of me and you.

But all that's left are shadows gray,
That linger on, they never stay.
The frost of fondness, a chilling truth,
The warmth we shared, the theft of youth.

Now solitude my only friend,
A heart once full, began to bend.
In the stillness, I hear the pain,
Of love remembered in the rain.

Memories in Every Corner

Dusty photographs line the walls,
Echoes of laughter, familiar calls.
In every room, a secret lies,
Unveiling truths behind our sighs.

The kitchen whispers of meals we shared,
In corners tucked, love declared.
Each trinket placed with tender care,
A testament to moments rare.

Sunlight dances on the floor,
As shadows weave through every door.
I close my eyes and hear a song,
Of cherished times where we belong.

The garden blooms with tales untold,
In vibrant hues, memories unfold.
And every flower, a reminder sweet,
Of simple joys, life's tender beat.

In every corner of this space,
A trace of you, a gentle grace.
Through time's embrace, I wander still,
Finding comfort in the thrill.

A Symphony of Absences

The notes of silence fill the air,
Composing sorrows, bare and rare.
Each heartbeat echoes, soft and low,
A symphony of what we know.

In vacant chairs, I feel the weight,
Of laughter lost, an aching fate.
The music plays, but none can hear,
The melody of love and fear.

Each empty room a haunting song,
Where memories linger, sad and strong.
In every pause, a story told,
Of heartstrings snapped, of hands let go.

Yet still I dance in shadows cast,
In rhythms of the fading past.
With every sigh, the strings do twine,
Creating harmonies divine.

For in this ache, a beauty glows,
A bittersweet that only grows.
Though absences may pierce the core,
A symphony of love endures evermore.

The Distance We Wove

In whispers soft, we spoke of dreams,
A tapestry of laughter seams.
Yet stars above, they drifted far,
As night concealed our shining star.

With every thread, a story spun,
The weaving done, but not the fun.
Each stitch a hope, a silent prayer,
Yet time pulled tight, took more than fair.

We walked the paths we once had known,
But shadows cast left us alone.
The distance grew, though hearts were close,
In threads now frayed, we learned the most.

The loom of life, it turned and swayed,
While colors bright began to fade.
In every knot, a lesson learned,
With each unravel, our hearts burned.

But still I find in dreams we weave,
A spark of hope, a chance to believe.
Though distances may stretch afar,
In threads of love, we'll find our star.

Echoes of What Was

In halls where laughter used to ring,
Now only echoes softly cling.
Memories dance on shadows' play,
Fading whispers call us to stay.

Photographs hang with dust and sighs,
Each image holds a thousand why's.
In moments passed, where joy once dwelled,
Echoes linger, love upheld.

Beneath the stars, we dreamt so bright,
Now lost in time's relentless flight.
The promises we once laid bare,
Are whispers tossed on evening air.

Yet in the silence, voices rise,
Like faded songs beneath the skies.
We gather threads of what remains,
A tapestry of gentle pains.

For though the past may slip away,
Its essence lingers, here to stay.
In every heart, an echo sounds,
Of love and loss that still surrounds.

Lost in the Silence

In quiet rooms where shadows creep,
The weight of silence, hard to keep.
Words unspoken hang in the air,
A haunting truth we cannot share.

The ticking clock, it marks the time,
While thoughts of you become my rhyme.
Each breath a pause, each glance a sigh,
In lovers' hearts, the dreams do die.

Moments fade as daylight wanes,
Emotions whirl like autumn rains.
In gazes cast, a story unfolds,
Of warmth once shared, now bitter cold.

Yet still I search for glimpses bright,
In shadows cast by fading light.
A spark of hope, a flicker near,
In silence lost, I'll persevere.

For even in the stillest night,
The stars above can offer light.
With every breath, I'll find a way,
To break the silence, come what may.

Frayed Connections

Like threads unraveled from a seam,
We wander lost, chasing a dream.
With every step, the bond grew thin,
In frayed connections, we begin.

A handshake meant to seal a pact,
Now echoes lost in time's cruel act.
The laughter shared, now memories fade,
In tapestry of losses made.

Yet in the fray, there's beauty found,
In raw edges, a new sound.
With every tear, the heart expands,
To gather hope with open hands.

In distances that stretch and bend,
We seek the light that never ends.
For though we're frail and worn with time,
In broken places, love can climb.

So let us weave with care and grace,
Embracing gaps that time must trace.
In frayed connections, let's ignite,
A spark of love to guide the night.

Sifting Through Echoes

In shadows deep we wander slow,
The whispers dance, a soft hello.
Memories drift like leaves in air,
Each one a story, silent, rare.

We sift through time, and pause to feel,
The weight of love, the cost of real.
In echoes past, we find our way,
A haunting song that starts to play.

The laughter lingers in the night,
A lingering ghost, a fleeting light.
In every sigh, a truth concealed,
In every heart, a wound revealed.

In twilight's glow, our shadows meet,
With every step, our hearts repeat.
We walk a line between the stars,
With every breath, we gather scars.

Through corridors of time we tread,
With all the dreams that lie unsaid.
Sifting through echoes, we will find,
The threads of fate forever bind.

The Spaces Where We Lingered

In quiet corners, love did bloom,
Where laughter echoed, chased the gloom.
We traced the paths of summer's day,
In every space, our hearts would lay.

Beneath the stars, our secrets shared,
In whispered tones, we both declared.
Those fleeting glances, soft as lace,
In timeless warmth, we found our place.

The old oak tree, the bench for two,
Where dreams were whispered, hopes were new.
We lingered long, in shadowed light,
In every touch, we felt the night.

The painted walls, the fading sound,
Of all the love, we've lost and found.
In every space, our laughter played,
In every pause, the memories stayed.

And as we drift from place to place,
The mark of joy, a soft embrace.
In all the spaces where we roamed,
In every heart, together homed.

A Palette of Silence

In hues of dusk, a silence speaks,
In gentle strokes, each moment peaks.
We paint the night with dreams untold,
In whispered tones, the brave and bold.

The canvas waits, the colors blend,
A sight of beauty we defend.
In every shade, a tale unfurls,
A quiet world of dreams and swirls.

With every brush, we shape the night,
In every hue, a glimpse of light.
We capture time in stillness rare,
A palette rich, beyond compare.

In muted tones, our spirits flow,
In every touch, a soft hello.
We find our voice within the calm,
A soothing balm, a healing psalm.

In the silence, beauty breathes,
In depths unseen, our spirit weaves.
With every stroke, we find our song,
In a palette rich, where we belong.

Threads of a Fractured Dream

In twilight's haze, the dream takes flight,
With threads of gold, and shadows slight.
We weave the night with hopes and sighs,
In every glance, a thousand cries.

The fabric frays, yet still we try,
To mend the seams, to reach the sky.
With every tear, a story sewn,
In fractured dreams, we find our own.

Amidst the chaos, colors bleed,
In every thread, a yearning seed.
We stitch our souls, with gentle care,
In every knot, a love laid bare.

The echoes whisper of what was lost,
In every thread, we pay the cost.
Yet through the pain, new patterns gleam,
In whispered hopes, we chase the dream.

As dawn approaches, shadows fade,
Yet in our hearts, the fabric's made.
With threads of light, we weave our theme,
In fractured paths, we form the dream.

Milton Keynes UK
Ingram Content Group UK Ltd.
UKHW020041271124
451585UK00012B/976

9 789916 899861